UNDERCURRENTS

UNDERCURRENTS

NEW VOICES

IN CANADIAN

POETRY

EDITED BY
ROBYN SARAH

Cormorant Books

The publisher gratefully acknowledges the support of the Canada Council for the Arts
and the Ontario Arts Council for its publishing program. We acknowledge the financial support
of the Government of Canada through the Canada Book Fund (CBF) for our publishing
activities, and the Government of Ontario through the Ontario Media Development Corporation,
an agency of the Ontario Ministry of Culture, and the Ontario Book Publishing Tax Credit Program.

Library and Archives Canada Cataloguing in Publication

Undercurrents : new voices in Canadian
poetry / Robyn Sarah, editor.

ISBN 978-1-77086-004-9

1. Canadian poetry (English)--21st century.
1. Sarah, Robyn, 1949–

PS8293.1.U53 2011   C811'.608   C2010-907931-0

Cover photograph and design: Angel Guerra/Archetype
Interior text design: Tannice Goddard, Soul Oasis Networking
Printer: Sunville Printco Inc.

Printed and bound in Canada.

CORMORANT BOOKS INC.
215 SPADINA AVENUE, STUDIO 230, TORONTO, ONTARIO, CANADA M5T 2C7
www.cormorantbooks.com

CONTENTS ⁓

UNDERCURRENTS

INTRODUCTION ～

Any poetry anthology is two things — a sampler of poets and a collection of poems — though the anthologist generally has one or the other foremost in mind. One type of anthology focuses on poets and seeks to define a group: poets of a particular region, poets of a generation, poets who share a demographic or cultural identity, poets of a movement or school, new poets, "best" poets. The second type of anthology focuses on poems, and the mandate is usually thematic (poems about love, poems about war, poems about parenthood or nature or the environment) — or formal (a collection of sonnets or haiku or a mix of traditional forms).

Both approaches have their pitfalls. The first anthologist may feel obliged to include some poets for their affiliations rather than for the quality of their poetry; the second may be tempted to include some less-than-excellent poems just because they fit the prescribed theme or form. Moreover, some poets and poems richly deserving of inclusion by the anthology's own mandate are bound to be missed because the anthologist doesn't know of them. (The proverbial first move of an anthology reviewer is to complain about who isn't in it: one title suggestion for this book, *Leafing Out*, was a non-starter because it sounded too much like "Leaving Out.") Yet, for all their inevitable shortcomings, anthologies are the mainstay and delight of serious readers of poetry. They are the fat volume that whets appetite for the slim volumes. They offer abundance without risk of monotony. They provide an overview, a smorgasbord, and the promise of surprise. They are, often as not, where we first encounter the poets who will be important to us, where we discover poets we would otherwise not know about, and where we first read the poems that become our personal touchstones.

Undercurrents: New Voices in Canadian Poetry is an introduction to the work of eleven Canadian poets who have not yet published full collections of their own (though most have published in magazines, both at home and internationally). In putting together a book of this nature, my thought was to include fewer poets but to give them each more space than the usual three to five pages one would expect in an anthology featuring new poets. I wanted generous selections that could give a real sense of each poet's range and vision. But I also wanted every poem to be a memorable poem, whatever its subject, style, or form. The idea was for this book to be first and foremost a collection of wonderful poems in its own right; secondarily, a harbinger for the poets' eventual debut collections.

I've long felt that chapbooks — mini-collections of ten or a dozen or fifteen poems, thoughtfully chosen and arranged — are the best introduction to an individual poet's work. Such little books have an intimacy to them; they invite more attentive reading than do full-length collections. There's a better chance that every poem will be read, that the poems will be read in sequence rather than by random flipping around, that they will be read more than once, and that the reader will come away having actually engaged with them and not just skimmed the surface. But besides being hard to distribute and get reviewed, chapbooks are ineligible for publishing subsidies and awards; not many publishers care to produce them. Most poetic debuts in Canada are full-length books, often over-long ones, competing for attention with new releases by established poets. Critics and poetry lovers alike despair of keeping up with them.

Undercurrents, then, was conceived not as a conventional sampler but more as a set of chapbooks. The contributors are all poets whose work I had come across (in magazines or elsewhere) whom I thought deserved attention in advance of their emergence, sooner or later, with books of their own. Each poet has ten pages, selected from a much larger body of work (often from a book-length manuscript in progress). I chose the poems both for their excellence as individual poems and for the ensemble they make, and I have sequenced each poet's selection, as far as possible, to work effectively as a suite.

Unlike most "new voices" anthologies, this one is not focused on a current generation of young poets — it does not equate "new" with "young." Nor is it age-restricted in any way. The contributors' ages span five decades, bringing to bear the perspectives and concerns of different life stages. There are many reasons why a poet may not publish a book early in life. Many fine poets write quietly for decades while making their careers elsewhere; if they do not publish a book when young, it may be harder to find a publisher later. Others, promising poets in their twenties, fall silent for long periods and only return to poetry later in life (this is especially true for women). Some only begin writing later in life, or switch genres from fiction to poetry later in life. Among these late bloomers may be found some of our more interesting and original poets, because they are not plugged into whatever's currently trendy in poetry; they find their voices independently, in solitude, uninfluenced by the stock tropes and conventions making the rounds of the MFA programs.

Why *Undercurrents*? The word bespeaks energy and movement beneath the surface, invisible yet significant movement, often pulling counter to the prevailing surface motion. There are, at any moment in a country's literary history, writers quietly at work who haven't surfaced yet, following their private inclinations and interests, moving in their own directions: the poets in this book, both young and older, come from this pool. But perhaps more saliently, one could say it is undercurrents that drive poetic practice in general and that characterize poetry as an art. Energy beneath the surface — of human consciousness, of human interaction, of the known and visible world — is what poets are drawn to explore; and energy beneath the surface of language, of words themselves, is what they draw on to explore it.

The undercurrents that tug at poets are various. Coming from different regions, different backgrounds and different walks of life, the poets in this volume have found hidden energy in dream, myth, philosophy and literature; in childhood memory, history and family history, geographies, and the mystique of place; in the dance of human connection, communal rites and the words that frame them; in the animal-vegetable-mineral permutations of nature and the seasonal dramas of rebirth and decay. Equally various are their ways of tapping into this energy: the musicality and lyricism of E. Blagrave and Sarah Feldman; Hamish Guthrie's spare yet humane directness; the formal deftness and allusive, brainy wit of Amanda Jernigan; Daniel Karasik's tonal balancing act between humour and gravitas; Michael Lithgow's stream of sensory impressions; George Pakozdi's mix of contemporary culture and echoes of the past; E. Alex Pierce's incantatory romanticism; Jason Rotstein's rule-bending experiments with idiom; Kay Weber's economy of expression and unerring expressive clarity; Margo Wheaton's feel for narrative and ear for local speech. Different as are these voices, they all explore our shared human condition in poems of lasting resonance — poems that invite reading aloud and stand up to re-reading, that balance sound with sense, that touch on universal situations and emotions and address them with depth, honesty, and beauty of language.

I could say more, but I don't want to mediate anyone else's experience of the poems collected here. Good poems speak for themselves. You are holding a book of them. Read and enjoy.

— *Robyn Sarah*
NOVEMBER, 2010

E. Blagrave

Eight Poems

Past Tense

His dream comes out at night;
a wanderer down a grey road
mistaken for somebody;
and suddenly the sharp smell
of the marsh.

She frightened four birds
in the rushes with her clear laugh.
The boat spun.
What finery — the bulrushes flashing.
The turtle brooded in the spin
and kept his silence.

The Sea Gull

There was once a sea-gull of green.

A bright night gull
fetching and coming in with the
logs shaken upon the tide.
He was like a light in the
harbours of houses.

The once timely branch made him a wing
buried in the air.
The once buried sword made him a beak
stirring the sun.
The grasses made him green.

The sea-gull moaned about these islands
like a parted wave;
grasping trees by their tops
with his yellow yellow feet.
We could seek his dismal shape
in the winds of kites.

He landed only in the marshes
near the windmill.
He greedily followed the sails.
The children would hunt
the marshes
to crack his emerald neck in two
or climb the windmill to break
the yellow claws,
while the sea-gull wailed over their hands.

The gull beat out to sea to come in
on the logs at night.
He was green like the sea weed.
His legs were yellow canes.

He is like the tide.
He gallops under the moon.
His groans are murderous.
His fishing loses ships.

I have penny-weights

I have penny-weights,
everyone.
I weigh stones that
men walk on.
I deal out the price of
coals
To warm such lame men's
bony souls.

this lame man had a treasure of stars
he forfeited all for one black coal
all he holds is a cinder of time

i keep those stars in a heap of fire
and measure them out on my penny-weight scale
i have reckoned their worth in terms of years
my diminished stars will be coals for hire

I have penny-weights,
everyone.
I weigh stones that
men walk on.
I deal out the price of
coals
To warm such lame men's
bony souls.

Chestnut and Grey

My horse has eyes like garnets,
    fiery under the moon.

Pony, trumpet for your love when
    the moon is full.

She's just a dark mare down in the
    dry shade breathing the
    scent of tumbleweed.

My horse has feet like thunder agates
    and he roars when the sun
    hits the plain.

Pony, call to your grey mare — she
    comes with a hide like glass.

Call to her when the moon is full
    and her eyes are as green
    as grass.

My horse, he's a thousand shades of red
    when the midwinter sun
    breaks the cloud.

Pony, here's your grey mare; she
    comes like a ghost,
    in foal.

Call to her when the moon is full
    and her eyes are beaten brass.

You are so alone

You are so alone in the next room.
The strings, the gentle creatures feed on air.
I stood by the cold window
and saw how the dark comes here.

The shapes of faces were everywhere
among the chimneys.
The sky was white with snow.
I saw one of its eyes through a chink
in a great wood wall.

On the south sides of buildings
the murk gathers in.

You sing one song.
I remember all this before.
It was going to be like this always.

The buildings are chained
and have in them lonely places.
The faces among the chimneys gather
with the snow, cloud and follow each
and one another here below.

Gatineau

A dove flew down
   like a cannonball bird
Mid-afternoon into
   Queen Anne's Lace.

Mid-afternoon
   among broken grass
   and golden stubble,
Haymakers humming
   to a hot blue sky,
I watch while a dove
   plays crazy,
   divebombing
   white flowers
   with a lunatic eye.

Bipolarities

i   The morbidity of
diminishing returns.
Dwarf and Giant
planted in flesh
complete and born
under the sun
where all things
normal
are busy with
all things normal.
But the shadows
cast by these
see-saw twins
straight from the womb
sun-spotted
clean to the bone
make us all, normally,
crooked as a thumb.

ii   We sail
like kites

in our dreams

landscaped
in streams of light;

a wavering gel
shimmering
in a cell-for-cell
trade-off
of lunar black
for lunar white.

iii   Chase, chase them away
        the ones who tell
        who catch you at it

    I live in a waterland
        mutable
    There's no place here
        for punctuation
        or truth
        only sleep
        and the cry of birds

    Perpendicular I am not
    No explanation

    Keep them away

iv   Stars break the sky,
        shiver into parts
        unseen by the
        human eye.

    When a child,
        I could hold
        one word, one day.

    Now words and days
        rattle in my hand
        and split into thousands.

Tilt

Tilt, the tumbling doves,
   white and grey
   among the green trees.

Tilt, a blind man's head,
   the whispering silk
   of his lady's dress.

Tilt, the hanged man's neck,
   the gingery root
   the sting of hemp.

Tilt, the knife edge of
   the axis, poling
   to antarctica.

Tilt, the random tiles
   out of the cup
Tilt, your face for
   a kiss.

ELIZABETH LOGAN BLAGRAVE was born in Edmonton in 1950. An air force brat, she lived on bases in Manitoba, Ontario, and Quebec before her father retired to Victoria. For six childhood years, "home" was her family's summer cottage in the Gatineau, a place she credits as having formed her. Beth began writing in her late teens, after hearing a recording of Dylan Thomas reading *Under Milk Wood*. Her twelfth grade English teacher, impressed with a paper she'd written on *The Waste Land*, exempted her from class, setting her up in a room with a typewriter. He also sent her to meet Robin Skelton, but she fled when Skelton, without warning or permission, began reciting her poems to assembled guests. At nineteen Beth moved to Montreal where she lived *la vie bohème* for a few fondly remembered years. Thirteen of her poems appeared in a single issue of *The Fiddlehead* in 1973, a print debut that apparently spooked her. Returning to Victoria, she worked for the government and as a sound and lighting technician for the Bastion Theatre. She began writing again in 2003 and has since published in *The New Quarterly*, *Arc*, *The Fiddlehead*, *The Antigonish Review*, and *Contemporary Verse 2*.

Sarah Feldman

Eight Poems

The Great Year

There is an old law, forged in the tuning of earth and sky
that nothing may come round in time except what holds
forever in the starry net of returns. If ever you lay in mothlit grass
saying whatever else you sang now, you'd sing to each other;
if once you felt the bow of stars arch up
under your breastbone and believed you were going there, if even once
you saw the skies align and time slide into joint — then yes, whatever
you sang you'll sing again, when the time flares once more with its unmaking,
bright hinge where intervening years are gathered as dead leaves
and cash for kindling.

These nights the skies are so clear, planets lined up for the perfect
shot, and your Venus among them, a sparkler of cold fire — it's almost possible
to imagine a world going on beyond us, intact. What one has understood
too early, too late, returns now in its time —
your long flight from on-the-other-hand, and the winding-up
felt in us down here, like the archer's readiness.
Ride the changes, you say. And I don't know, I don't know,
but every year come October I'm on my way again
to what we've missed in these bright paths
of falling and flight, here where all the lights
align into a single shining, where all our arrows sing together
on one arc the same whether we are coming or going,
leaving, being left.

October

The earth is dying. Some core of sustaining fire has failed in her,
the last of its heat and light running out in currents
that surge and short like power in a broken grid.

Meanwhile the season goes on in its passion-play —
the low sun ignites the maples in a corona of fire
the leaves shiver and blaze with the annunciatory fever
of a death and transformation no warm-blooded thing will ever know.

And yet some false note is struck — our joy in the changing lights
and technicolour dawns seems forced now, overblown.
Even our grief is wrong, our tears too fluent,
a rhythm as ancient and even as the tree's unleaving,
as if there were no difference in this late sickness, this rot
as faultless as the living root breaking down the dead.

The earth is dreaming, like a dying man who dreams he is a child
weeping inconsolably over some lost bright thing; who wakes, dry-eyed
with no sound for the claws that twist in him.

Elegy for Dizzy the Cat

It is because you have no soul,
only this manyness, a trick
of making the body multiple and slipping as smoke
so that no door or crack or crevice remains impenetrable,
no pleasure unsurrendered-to, no anxious hand
secure you against abandonment, because no one
ever taught you the gates of true and false sleep, their infinite
divisions and late late fulfillments, there is now no name
that would give you back to yourself, no words
that might remember for you in an unimaginable time and place
no elsewhere, no special place in my heart forever,
your going now to us unknowable,
a door shut on a love that loved with all the surface of its skin.

Black Bile

I

I am not myself. Days pass; I write them off.

Someone else, it must be, writes me back
into the Book of Life each morning,
signs my name in x's.

I sit in the sun. Spring comes, knuckle by knuckle,
buds pressing out, dogwood blooming in white fists.

Walks in the courtyard, watched over by a dull inquisitor
who asks, over and over, one question, always unanswerable, *Where
does it hurt?*

Pain is elsewhere — in the face of my inquisitor,
endlessly patient, scrupulously blank,
in the shuffle of the old man who goes so slow
in his daily crossing of the grass, his whole being
distilled into the ache and heft
of one more step.

Or else what? There is nothing left to write off.
There are bits of sunlight glittering in the grasses,
grey-blue edges piling on the horizon.

Worse days are coming. Gather up your bed.
You can stand more than you think, more than you want to think.

II

Is this the bottom? But there's no rest here.
Each morning you make again your sleepless bed
folding clean sheets over the narrow strait
where you twist each night as on a grill.

Breakdown? What is that? Each morning you tie back your hair
and walk the halls. Under the long, bleared windows of the dayroom
you sit blinking and peeling an orange. You sit you stand answer
to your name when called, still bent
whole under the gestures that broke you.

Yet still you are one of the lucky ones, you can look out the window.
Above the brick-and-glass complex, a perfect summer blue —
cloudless, without secrets. There's nothing for you there.
Beyond the concrete horizon, it all leaks away,
and whatever it is you wanted —
an extra sleeping pill, some new song
to get you through the night — is nowhere.

The strong, blank sunlight floods the dayroom.
You take it in like a bitter placebo.

Four a.m. The clock tower

Four a.m. The clock-tower calls the hours in the empty street.
Again, again, again, again. I wake to nothing, my heart overbeating

Like a punctual mistake; a bulb, overwintered, waking
to the sun of a summer already passed.

We are strangers. You are someone passing my window on your way.
I love you — an indiscretion for which I am, mostly, forgiven.

And yet your eyes still seek out mine — in boredom, or accident,
or the mild cat-and-mouse play of desire — in passing.

We are strangers. Our back windows share a view
of the same crumbling graveyard, the hills covered in waves

Of unnameable wildflowers, evening slanting down
from the brush at the edge of the hill, the same capricious

Play of unseasonable light and rain. The same knowledge
of a winter that does not yield to the rhythms of passing time; the shock

Of unaccountable spring parting the snow-locked distance
like a useless miracle. There's no help, now,

In crying out to the solitary street — if I called out your name
there would only be my own voice going on in the dark

With no echo. My heart still beating beyond me,
for no reason, blow after blow.

Lie quiet now. This passes, as the snow passes,
and the rain that weights the petals and the wind

That tears them from the stem, as the light that wakes
them to a promise that can only break, and break —

Passes on and on — and into what? You are no one,
anyone, passing my window, hour after hour.

But who am I, just now awakened, stricken down to the nerve-root
by some tremor already passed before my eyes had opened

To say what it is that passes, or whose heart
will be returned to me from the ceaselessly beating leaves, whose cries

Open my mouth, when it has passed?

Acheron (from "Letters for the River")

> *People do not understand how that which is at variance with itself agrees*
> *with itself. There is a harmony in the bending back, as in the case of the*
> *bow or the lyre.*
> — Heraclitus

Do you know, when you left
I went down and drank the grey
dregs where the sand and water mix
there at the edge, where the heart
unsticks like a drain and the dishslop of used
time leaks away, sloshes in
and leaks away. And even then
you came back sometimes when the wind
came up off the water towards evening — or no, still nothing
but the daymoon in the sky and the one who lives in your
death and dies in your life, singing *Down*
into the tides of thirst, swept out clear to Lethe.

I just wanted to say that everything
is okay here; that the parts
you didn't send arrived safely and I hope
you're safe too, whatever you've decided
that means. I've finally stopped asking
about my letters, and even if it's true it just gets harder
and harder to find a word you'd trade against silence —
did you know? — all this time away you've been teaching me
the language of herons, lichen, driftwood —

It's dusk here, then night falls
then dusk again, time neither
an arrow nor a circle, but like a bow bent back to almost
breaking. My letters float back along the waves,
soaked, illegible; signs.

Scherzo, *Do I remember spring* (from "Kore")

Do I remember spring? I remember dropped flowers in some field
and two or three weeks I thought would come again
as if my heart was a tulip bulb, trembling up
out of its underground cell each time certain
conditions recurred: April, the spray of blossoms
stippling the lawn, marbled skies where starlings
disperse and gather in shifting knots —
I remember a passage of light so full and speaking
even its hesitations seemed meant, as grace notes —
so that, as time passed, the usual figures assembling and dissembling,
I sensed none of the usual lack, as if one right gesture might release a person
from the need to break off, repeat. So that the end,
when it came, found me waiting: out on the swept porch, I watched
the stars come out one by one, the fixed
and perfect form of every scattering, and could not think
of a single wish left in me,
even the wish for more time.

Coda, *When we had outwalked ...* (from "Kore")

When we had outwalked the last trace of earth and body's heat
and still the fields stretched out before us, like the long day's
current running on through sleep; then my companion,
who had gone all this way by my side without one word
of comfort or reproach, turned to me, saying *Sing something.*
By which he seemed to mean the way is long —
we would not reach the end of it — but no, not infinite.
Even now a space was being made where I could rest,
there, in eyes in which the distances come clear.
How can I say we are not given our full measure, only because it is nowhere,
unless here, in our seasons' unimaginable ratio? I was about to sing —
of swept fields laid out to where they waken gold in the late sun,
of a blue so clear the birds vanish into it, always some two or three
bright seeds that flare and fail and never touch the earth —
when I met your eyes a second time, asking,
How long do we have?

SARAH ELIZABETH FELDMAN was born in 1982 in Nashville, Tennessee to Canadian parents, and grew up in Iowa City, Iowa, and London, Ontario. Though technically a dual citizen, her language is firmly grounded in the accents of the CBC, with a special mastery of the random and compulsive "I'm sorry." At eighteen, she moved to British Columbia, studying creative writing and philosophy at the University of Victoria, and publishing poems in *Grain*, *The Fiddlehead*, *The New Quarterly*, *The Malahat Review* and *The Antigonish Review*. She still calls British Columbia home. She received an M.A. in philosophy from Dalhousie, but her uncontrollable giggling during seminars dissecting the semantic import of the phrase "lemons are yellow," and an inability to understand a word of her own finished thesis, suggested an unfitness for the academic world. At twenty-four she ran away to the East Village, New York, to become a rock journalist, writing reviews and interviews for *Popmatters*, *The Villager*, *Chelsea Now*, and *ArtistDirect*. At twenty-five she vanished down a rabbit hole, and eventually resurfaced in London, Ontario, where she is completing a memoir of tea parties in Avernus.

Hamish Guthrie

Nine Poems

Christmas

The jets' rush starts this miracle: we fly,
lift-off of a hundred tons,
so many we could be a little town,
cradled in aluminum.

We eat peanuts in the sky.
We fall asleep
between the earth and moon.

We drop at night like angels
into Minneapolis, that lies
like a million scattered
candles in the snow.

The Bubble's Hold

Inside his jacket
a quilt of wires plugged him into heat
in the tight, clear bubble of the gun
at 20,000 feet.
Tonight brings back
the sudden fate he wore,
the engines' heavy rumble
toward the target,
the anti-aircraft guns that tried to pick
a father out of this
mission to a foreign city,
him, eighteen, over Czechoslovakia,
the moment no one could pull out,
the wing-to-wing formation fixed —
death, breaking it, as easy as the flak
through glass.
It held. The sky's fire died.

The story ruined
a ball-bearing factory,
and carried him to Europe
in the belly of a plane
that nightmares crashed,
when, warnings to evacuate ignored,
the city, reinforced, fired back.
The odds were even in his dream,
but the story stacks the odds for death.
The kitchen counter shatters with black flak.

Something unzipped this
tonight. I try to hear his guns.
He lost the jacket fifty years ago,
but the noise comes home,
explosions, and the
mercy of the glass that held him
and did not break.

A Road Near Kosovo

They walk toward us
beside thick trees,
along a road the paper says
has emptied fields and towns.
A family, a fragment of the line,
a man and wife, holding, between them,
a large cloth bag.

They have clearly only started out.
Nothing has tousled, yet,
the woman's neat blond hair,
as chic as if it had been styled today.
Two children run and laugh,
as if this line,
in heat that's stripped
an old man to his undershirt,
were tourists headed for the beach.

The camera leaves them
lurching further into this,
toward what camp they find,
in lightweight shoes
and summer clothes,
and not much else for the sun
or worse weather,
days more like this ahead,
naked to the stones
of shifting policy
and the rains of diplomacy,
between them, a large cloth bag
getting heavier
with everything they left behind.

Geography

I hear he's failed geography.
The rivers of the world
run on in emptiness to him,
and all the complicated names
for rock are meaningless.

But I have seen him, slouching at his desk,
open chasms in himself
like continents,
oblivious to me or anyone.
He's learned the way
the heart of things can boil
and harden into shape,
how islands are defined.
He's felt words like a river's push
gain force
and carry everything away.

His white Crown Royal baseball cap
screens more than rain or sun.
But I have seen him sit
for half an hour with a book
about a boy whose family
is broken into splinters of grey rock,
and read until he finds a place inside the world,
and one long river that he knows.

In Country Near Elora

This air
is the breath
of tomatoes
and timothy grass.
A stream divides
cattle pasture
from fields.
The water slows
at a pool
and goes under the road.
Red-winged blackbirds
in the reeds
chatter and fuss.

On circling currents,
hawks rise
and decline.
The hills are fat
with the heaviness
of corn
and dust.
Cattle turtle
into the shade.
White butterflies
migrate
across alfalfa.

The lane
falls asleep
at noon.
It waits,
beside the barn,
for the bone white footsteps
of the moon.

The Afterlife

The afterlife, do you believe in it?
he asked. The topic came up at the bar.
This deepened the agenda
on a snowy night.
One of us wished to believe,
like his parents. One of us
was categorical. You die, that's it, you're done,
carbon in the ground. Proved this with a story,
said he put his father's ashes in the ground,
felt nothing, lowered the urn, set him down,
felt no electric flash.
This stilled the beer at our lips.
They took my silence
for agreement. I leaned back,
wanting hope, but remembered
my own cold mornings
inside a cemetery's gates,
but could not, somehow, then
give an account of this.
Death seemed a good long stretch
from where we were that night,
and if, for me,
the moment was a muted podium,
I relished, in the noisy interference all around me,
the distance to the final, lettered stone.
Relished also, that cold night,
the ease of ordering one more
by raising my empty bottle.

The Castle

The road he took
from an ancient city
was longer and more difficult
than marked on the maps:
the curling route to the coast,
the sudden jump across the Atlantic.
Arrival was a long descent;
his clothes weren't right for the climate.
He looked back too often
for escape to be easy, and the stones
of that city became things he carried.
Memory took him back to flag-stoned chambers
and lifted down the trophies on the walls.
Sickness sometimes affects rough settlements
in a new country, and he was not immune.
The past, like a virus in his blood, gave him
a fever like the illness bones take
from cold stone buildings. He described
the dogs he followed on the Braid Hills,
the tents he pitched at Comrie, fires
where the boy poached kippers.
He needed the rain where he was born,
the rock that choked the centre of that city,
wet roads he walked to school. His head
was full of photographs we could not see,
and looking at them divided him from us.
When I was born, I was the son
he could not show his father.
I feared the castle that he left
as a cold place locked in his head.
I looked for the door he had opened
when he left, and could not close.

Night Fishermen on Bronte Pier

The old wharf drowned.
Fish-boats in the twenties
unloaded trout and salmon
ice-packed to New York,

the sagging pier
awash in gutted slime.
Now the developers
moor condominiums.

A gallery has drifted in,
and next door, patrons
in a bar watch the lake
and drift out on good wine.

You can buy lingerie
on the new river,
and papier maché parrots
nest in a boutique.

But on the pier, at one a.m.,
a Tuesday in November,
nothing floats
except the wrinkled moon.

On canvas stools
wrapped shapes in parkas
trade cigarettes
and fish the huddled dark.

Their sport is the sun's
antithesis.
They sink into
the moon's uncertainties

that promise nothing
but lumpish freighters
crawling the horizon.
Jokes bait the air,

and cigarettes throw wide
a moment's net
of smoke that hangs
then dissipates.

Time swims away.
They count the night
in silvers, if there's luck,
hours, if there's not.

In willow breaks
along the shore
the night wind sags.
They may take nothing more.

Noise

My neighbour's restless.
He's built a shed, a deck,
and now a wooden fence.
His wild saw screams.
Banging nails annoy the shrieking birds.
Our flowers bloom beside this factory.

I know the reason why.
Winter wrecked him twice:
two deaths: his son, by suicide,
and then his brother. We heard,
and wondered what grief did,
those slow, grey months that kept us all inside.

He's making something out of this.
Leans on the fence to talk about his shed,
his metal saw. I'm with the shrieking birds,
but I admire the work we hear,
the nails he buries in new wood
between our properties.

HAMISH GUTHRIE was born in Toronto in 1952. His father read poetry aloud at family meals — Coleridge, Hardy, Burns; other early influences were the *Faber Book of Modern Verse*, a high school teacher at Upper Canada College who had the class memorize all the major speeches in Hamlet, and discovering John Berryman's *Dream Songs*. (An elegy Hamish wrote for Berryman was published in the U.S. when he was twenty-three.) Studying English and philosophy at the University of Toronto's Victoria College, he found Northrop Frye's course on Tudor poetry particularly memorable. Hamish travelled in England, France and Scotland as a boy and again after university, walking a long stretch of the Pennine Way, moor country of northern England. Working summers for the old Lands and Forests department in Ontario, he explored the country around Parry Sound and much further north, and with his Montana-born wife, acquired a love of writers and places of the west. Since 1976 he has taught at White Oaks Secondary School in Oakville, Ontario, where he heads the English department and has coached drama, soccer, and debate.

Amanda Jernigan

Nine Poems

Off-Season

I rest the sword across my knees
and lean against the garden gate.
I check my pocket for the keys.
The trees are heavy with their fruit.

You may discern, at orchard's end,
by what scant light the moon affords,
two meagre figures, hand in hand,
diminishing horizonwards.

Peopled, Eden was, it's true,
a pleasant park in which to ramble;
I myself once found it so.
But empty it's a better symbol.

Adam's Prayer

In the sweat of thy face shalt thou eat bread:
you put this rather beautifully,
and gave me leave to sing my work
until my work became the song.

In sorrow shalt thou eat of it:
a line on which a man might ring
the changes as he tills the ground
from which he was taken. Thistle, thorn

(in the which is the fruit of a tree yielding seed),
these too shall it bring forth to thee,
all the days of thy life till the end,
the synagogue of the ear of corn.

Poem and plowman cleave the dark.
One can't eat art. But dust is art,
and unto dust shall I return.
O let my song become my work.

Lullaby

My little lack-of-light, my swaddled soul,
December baby. Hush, for it is dark,
and will grow darker still. We must embark
directly. Bring an orange as the toll
for Charon: he will be our gondolier.
Upon the shore, the season pans for light,
and solstice fish, their eyes gone milky white,
come bearing riches for the dying year:
solstitial kingdom. It is yours, the mime
of branches and the drift of snow. With shaking
hands, Persephone, the winter's wife,
will tender you a gift. Born in a time
of darkness, you will learn the trick of making.
You shall make your consolation all your life.

Holy

The words the weight of a stylus only,
travelling the surface slip
of clay, make slight impressions when
you hear them first. Repeated, they
cleave to the groove. This is the source
of faith; the words ring true. When Hamlet
walks on stage, act three, scene one,
the audience inhales en masse
and mouths, 'To be, or not to be ...'.
Thus, even unbelieving, I
recite in earnest, 'And it came to pass
in those days that there went out a decree
from Caesar Augustus.' Travelling home,
we likewise cleave to roads we know,
and in our minds the tracks are laid
for these small houses letting go
of smoke, these rivers clenched
in ice, these pockmarked signs,
and whether there's a child or not,
the roads run thick with traffic, lines
of people going to be counted.

Marrying Days

These, my friends, are marrying days.
One afternoon last summer I saw
my childhood orchard fortress made
a wedding bower, and my erstwhile
ally of those boy-girl wars go bearing
the white standard, happily, to hold
a parley with the gentleman opposed.

Two other friends, in March, took hands
and swore, in the parlance of our times,
to live together, after Customs
and Immigration's ordinance,
in the holy estate of modern love,
and in so doing named each other
person and person, if not man and wife.

Now you. I wonder: what words
will you choose to be the footmen
of your vows, of all words? In what costume
will you wed? What dignitaries will preside
at this your co-ordainment? To whom
shall I address this poem? To whom
it may concern: that is, to you.

May you be, not of one mind, but mindful
of each other; not of one flesh, but, fleshly,
may you delight in one another.
May you be, not of one heart, but heartily
in love, for all your days; and may
we count among your blessings, ever,
this your love not born but made.

The Marble King of Athens, Greece

Mibless, he borrowed his first shooter —
from the son of an air-force man, who loaned
it grudgingly and lived to rue it —
then captured every marble he would own.
The local urchins, army brats,
suspendered sons of diplomats,
in the Attic sun they knuckled down
and played for keeps.

Knock a marble from the ring,
keep the marble, shoot again.
Hit your partner's taw instead,
and take his mibs for he is dead.

He tallied up his victories:
the swirls and agates, steelies, all
those cat's-eyes, crystals, potteries,
the corns and big dough-rollers,
an embarrassment of riches. Now
he spills them out to see them, how
each one contains in its keel
a scrap of light;

now he consigns them to their sack.
He trusts them to a steamer chest
of linens which, by luggage rack
of army jeep, is taken to the USS
America. The crossing takes
a week. Back home, when he unpacks
the chest, he rifles through the sheets
and finds them gone.

Were they stolen by a docker?
Or taken as a tar's reward
and anted up in steerage poker?
Or by a guileful cabin steward
as ransom for this voyage to his son?
Perhaps just lost. Well, he won
them once and he can win them over
again, he thinks. In dreams, however,

he sees the satchel, sinking, helped
undone by currents, sow its prize
in coral reefs and groves of kelp
till those that were his pearls are eyes.

Memoir

I thought about a narrow road.
At length, it stretched before me.
I travelled it, unravelled it:
it seemed to ravel from me.

At first it was a simple line
and then it was a circuit
and then it seemed to spiral inwards —
farther still I took it.

It seemed to lengthen under me.
It offered no encounter.
Diminishing circumferences
contracted to a centre.

I found a mighty crossroads there,
twelve byways intersecting.
I set up as a customs guard,
a heavy toll collecting.

Now days and nights I've bided here
and sometimes I imagine
I'm coextensive with the web,
so close its oscillation:

myself become circumference,
attending radii
within, and at my centre something
tugging like a fly.

Catch

My father was holding a ball in the shape
of the sun. The sun,
he said, at four point five
billion years of age, is in its prime:
with more or less an equal span ahead
before, its hydrogen depleted,
it begins to slough its shells and eat
its children, a red
giant. By which time
you, my son, and I will be long gone, and all we love.
And then he tossed the ball to me. I didn't mean
to catch it but my hands reached up.

Blackout

Wartime, the city under blackout, you had to trust
that what you'd seen by day would be enough
to help you find your way by night, dead reckoning down Water Street,
to the place where the laneway ended, the right door opened.

Exactly so I've seen you feel your way along
a line of verse, inserting *something something*
for the trochees that you knew were there, until you reached the rhyme-word
at the end. Now, of course, the city

is under blackout. What we know now of your life
is all we'll ever know: we have to trust
that it's enough to help us find our way down *something something* streets
to the place where something ends and something opens.

AMANDA JERNIGAN was born in Kitchener-Waterloo, Ontario, in 1978, into a family of readers and writers. Her grandfather, a Washington D.C. newspaper man, delighted in reading poetry out loud (Hodgson, Daly, Riley, Whittier, Tennyson, Kipling, Coleridge, Yeats), leaving her entranced, from early on, with the aural qualities of language. Amanda has studied English literature at Mount Allison University, Memorial University, and McMaster University, where she is currently embarked on a doctoral degree. In 2002/2003, she interned as Publishers' Assistant to Tim and Elke Inkster at Porcupine's Quill. She has subsequently worked as a literary editor for Porcupine's Quill (most recently on *The Essential Richard Outram*, 2011), as well as for Anchorage Press, Gaspereau Press, and the literary journals *The New Quarterly* and *Canadian Notes & Queries*. She has worked as a performer and playwright with DaPoPo Theatre (Halifax and Berlin), and has taught in the English departments at Memorial and Mount Allison universities. Amanda's poems have been published in Canada, the U.S., and Belgium, and are represented online in the archive of the Poetry Foundation. *Groundwork*, her first book of poems, is forthcoming from Biblioasis in 2011. She lives in Hamilton, Ontario, with her partner, the artist John Haney.

Daniel Karasik

Ten Poems

Conditions

So the great negotiator atop the mountain
there equivocated. All this is fine,
he said, that it should be as a dream
is fine — but now you will
accept
my conditions:

that it should be as a dream
held always on the precipice
before waking;
and that we, the dreamers,
should be as children
laughing in their sleep.

Union Station

Raise up the storied ceiling high
for the swift impressioning of visitors: let voices echo
in bronze chambers of arrival, in which the names,
stone-graven, of the country's gods
stare down, each letter with gravity observing
the passing and entering of downcast eyes.

Here is a hall that says: *Without
is grandeur, empire.* And the visitor nods.
And, says the hall, in the breathing silence
of the highest of its airy spaces,
*it is always dawn, promising and promised,
without.*

The visitor takes her bags and leaves, goes forth
into the hazy brightness of morning, into air moist
with spit from cabbies' trumpets.

The city wakens, watches, calculates.

Twelve Amnesiacs

1

Twelve amnesiacs sit down
to write their autobiographies.

2

Twelve   sit down
    write their autobiographies. They
        lacking in   and
labels.   a dictionary?
Or, for   sake, some photos?

3

Twelve autobiographies sit down
to redefine amnesia. My life was filled
with spotty remembrances, says one.
Does that count? I forgot everything
my wife said about money, says another.
May that be included
under the definition?

4

Twelve strangers, some knowing
who they are, some entirely confused,
sit down with a pad of blank paper.
By the end of the evening they are friends.
Some have had children together.
But don't ask them to tell you
how it happened,
what they live for.

If carefully your father sat

If carefully your father sat
on the edge of a bed
at the late hour when clocks
fly home to tend to lovers' arms

and dizzy children;
if carefully you sat beside him
and were shocked and shivery,
not for the first time,

to hear his heart beating;
if I asked you to meet me at the bus station
so that together we might make our escape and not grow
fragile like our parents,

would you?

I wondered this shortly after listening
to my mother's soulful and gentle 2 a.m. pulse,
was reminded of it when I noticed
that the sound of your ragged breath while sleeping

ebbs with a cadence
no different.

I listened carefully, delicately,
knowing the whole thing could break at any moment —

The Scholar

It seemed easy, and we seized the task as soon
as we felt ready. Caring was all, they said,
you have only to care a lot, about *one* thing:
and to build it up with the words that caring owns.

But then the confusion. The great houses that our caring
afforded us, the sharp wine, the safety after
what seemed, in the mind's youth, such endless descent.

So that we were not sure, later, if we cared
at all, or if we'd simply conned the rhythms
that convince.

    And that's not me.

            I'd rather
care in the cold, alone, or dreaming naked
in a quiet place at least. I'd rather care
with plaintive cry: hear me, hear me! (— above
the hum of secret suns burning leagues deep
beneath the city...)

Old Men Running

I have brushed hands and towels
with aged naked men
at the gym, staying fit
in the nightcap of their lives
by pushing Newtonian laws of motion
to absurd extremes, and not covering up
anything,
at all,
ever.

They share a camaraderie with each other; perhaps
some fought a war together and now
they're sharing a row of lockers, a little slice of quiet glory
down from the track.

I have noticed, and I will beg you not to share this,
that my abdominal and pectoral muscles
are both more taut than theirs
and more well-defined.

I cannot figure out the schematic by which this is justified:
I have not earned anything;
I am not so old as to have deserved my youth.

But there is some balance in the fact that
no old man has ever smiled kindly at me there,
which tells me, primarily, lewd thoughts aside,
that they know nothing I don't.

From this I derive comfort
and a fear that drives me
to run
faster than all of them.

Dusk

The evening shift comes on; an apron
hung on its hook. Minutes she spends
in the kitchen, then reappears plainclothed
with her dinner.

And all the chairs
are still. Breeze, a fine dust
entering from the patio.

She can breathe a minute, her pasta hot,
before the rush, the men,
the loud.

Her hair tied up.
A stranger, maybe,
will lunge and need her in the evening;
but one who knew her
would embrace her now.

Sanctity

It is not holy if you tell it
to a stranger
on the beach.

It cannot be holy
if it is a story whose telling
has become habitual,
I met her in the shade,
she wore green,
inclined her head a bit,
we'd gone to the same school
but never met.

It is coarse, it is crude,
it is profane and it does no favours
to the millions who wait
knowing or unknowing
for what is holy,
for what is secret,
for what can be told only in fragments,
reluctantly,
to old drunks and grandmothers
on buses,
barely listening.

Young Lovers, Afternoon Café

Dressed up and groomed neat
but the eyes betray him: flitting,
furtive, squirrelly. Tie a little loud.
And the knee jerk. And the foot tap.

She clasps his hand on the table,
binds him fast and roots him
to the earth.

She will be width to his narrow,
earth to his air and fire, and fire
to his swift waters.

Should he build a house, should he be a builder,
she'll be the house: his ideal, constructed
with breath.

If she is the one who makes music,
he'll be the music: her fingers on him,
her artfulness more theirs than hers.

There they will sit till due autumn,
till the squirrel climb out of him
and the lion roar in, and the bear, and the ox,

heavy moving nature of hunt and rest
and long labour. And there she will grow wiser,
and grip him tighter, make beds and lunch and coffee,

and the wild storm she contains grow wilder and wilder.

Others Will Be Remembered

Others will be remembered who sing of the blackness only.
Others whose visions are of a long day's road
out in a cold storm at dark swiftly ending
without song or love or sense:
they'll sing of this,
and they'll be remembered.

No matter. Carry on, tighten the straps on your bag
stuffed till seams' breaking, wear appropriate clothes
in spring and in winter, noticing the weather,
the flowers and their dying, men and women
at work in their fields and asleep in their towers,

dreaming of rainfall,
and the storm's last amber,
and the quiet, after,
from which your song, the other kind,
unnoticed rises.

DANIEL KARASIK was born in Toronto in 1986 and grew up in the suburbs north of that city. He began writing poetry in high school, probably as a result of reading poets like Alden Nowlan, Anne Carson, and Rainer Maria Rilke, and thinking they were on to something. In his first year at the University of Toronto, he had the opportunity to study with poet A.F. Moritz, a particularly rewarding experience. Since his mid-teens Daniel has spent much time working in professional theatre and in the film and television industry, as a writer and an actor. His play *In Full Light*, published by Playwrights Canada Press, has been presented in Toronto, New York City, and Potsdam, Germany (in German translation). His poems have appeared in journals and he was a first place winner of the *Toronto Star*'s poetry contest. In 2006 Daniel travelled extensively through West Africa and Israel, volunteering at a cultural centre in the east of Ghana, studying at a yeshiva in Jerusalem, and doing other, less purposeful things. Daniel has frequently if inconsistently been a student at the University of Toronto, studying philosophy and literature.

Michael Lithgow

Ten Poems

loss

Speak slowly at first so that the words can find
their moments of disbelief. Every syllable
is a kind of hunger with tendrils reaching
from the messy mathematical soil of your memory
to your need. Be prepared to flinch,

let some of the words crack the glass face
of the present. The tendrils also touch
the future. Sometimes a beautiful sound. One of sorrow's chimes.

because of the light

It sounded like applause, and then he counted the leaves —
there were nine, a small cluster on a large branch

over a streetlight on an otherwise barren tree. What made him
stop, what made him change, was the leaves were clinging

to the light, were clinging because of the light, and nine lives
had to be considered. He remembered a thunderstorm

and the sound frogs make squeezed in the hand, and bumblebees
in a honeysuckle bush — there were others: the way a worm flinched

on a fishhook, bones and down like gimcrack in grass
beneath an eagle nest, the lightness of a turtle's vertebrae,

a dessicated mole, a dying cat and a moth wriggling for days
in a spider's web by his window. He could count

nine breaths, and hold his breath for nine seconds.
How many lives was he made of? He once

held nine marbles in his mouth. His knowledge, of course,
was limited. This time, it was the leaves who held their breaths,

or they were breaths, or were running out of breath. He could hear it.
It was late, dry leaves scraping in circles on an empty street,

now and then a car passing, the occasional wind-bang
of a shutter startling cats. And so he walked, his memory

of thunder urging him along, counting his breaths
under the light that bends even the filaments of trees.

the desire of everything

What was the fascination with fire
telling us? A crackling in the heads

of 11 year olds, stuffing ping-pong balls
with matches, igniting words

written in mud, on sidewalks, in sandboxes
with butane, watching something alive burn

from dead grass. There was a recipe
for gunpowder, kitchen alchemy with sulfur

scraped from match tips and burnt wood
and sugar and saltpetre in a bowl,

moving the metal spoons slowly. I loved
that my fingers could snap ghosts from almost anything,

that liquids burned, that *we* could burn and watch
our fingers in flames like Johnny Torch — *flame on*!

before burying our hands in the sand.
I loved that we could reach past ourselves with gestures

as sublime and ridiculous as we were, that we held a key
to a pleasing secret. I liked it more than smallness

and boredom, more than my room, more
than my paper route. A lot more than my paper route.

More than discovering a world of exhaustion,
of people who spelled magic wrong — I mean,

who spelled it in a way that didn't spell
the desire of everything (almost everything)

to *burn, burn, burn.*

the lives of shadows

I noticed my arms hanging
from my shadow as if pinned at the shoulder.
I was walking home from yet another goodbye.
I was behind a man, and it was my shadow
he could see stretching in the front,
my dangling arms a little ghoulish. He was
limping and moved to let my shadow pass.
Instead, it walked at his side for three blocks
asking for mercy. Under the bridge,
as usual, I could see that the shadows
were men slumped into the concrete.
My shadow ignored them.

I'm still unsure how to say goodbye.
This was a 6.5 — I've taken to rating them
like a skating judge. After,
I sat in the bar alone, so alone
the barman came to tell me *his* story, not
a bad one, about old sofas decorated with
Haida carvings and soda signs from Chinese
cafés — *the decor of the bar* — a man

who collects and must live with that sadness.
Then I watched the light in the bar stuff itself
into empty glasses on tables. I watched a man
and woman try to dance on separate bar stools
while their shadows touched at my feet.
I watched myself walk home, tired of trying to say
goodbye, tired of watching my shadow beg.

God knows, the lives of shadows must be hard.

birthday at the beach

Ten tankers in the port stopped in a stone grey
rain. I take ten small steps beside sea-retch,
broken shells, and seaweed ruined in the sand.

There are houses here, too, and they steal from me:
a great pretending, as if this place could be exalted
with a price. The whispering I hear

is more than I can stand — gods and fleas banging around
on the sand in the scummy foam, bones and bleached trash,
perfect remnants of a bad dream. An eagle plays in the air

tearing somersaults in the wind with talons bared
and beak open, barking over the ocean's soft metal
and it folds my heart in two, then four, then six

then eight, like a tiny origami anchor.
I can imagine days — *not mine*, but in a better
dream, that spill from the sun almost like wax

and harden under the seal of our footsteps.
I love you, and I must leave. It's sad, and angry,
and an almost perfect celebration of a birthday.

a child sleeps on the bus

A child sleeps on the bus with his mouth slightly open.
Crowded around him are men and women in parkas;
confusion, sleepiness and isolation are like a cloudy
light. Morning rush. There is a bit of dream in the air,
and the hard eyes of a poor man are cast down
into the gravel and debris on the floor. Everywhere

there are sleeping giants. The boy is dreaming that he is
everywhere. When the bus bangs on the road his eyes flutter,
open momentarily, then close. It is hard enough
to dream on a bus. The windows are splattered with dry salt.
The confusion is not so hard to understand, like tumbling
in dreams. We make sense of it until we wake.

The morning light pries. The bus heaves with the lights,
bodies jostle one against the next, they touch,
everywhere flicked eyes and heads look away
refusing this intimacy. The dream of the boy changes,
loses its shape, opens. There is a snarl of sound,
the bus machinery grinding us down, traffic gunning

on the road, a kind of churning. Down goes up
when you fly in a dream, your body becomes light
and you float and travel so long as confusion
and dread don't break through, and everywhere
you find memory, patterns that are yours. Open a door
and your childhood pops out. The dream

has a lurching rhythm of its own, a jumble.
The boy's dream fills the bus, reaches out through tiny
fibrils of light touching everyone. Even when his eyes
open we remain delicately entwined. Even the man
with the downcast eyes is touched by the light, a bag of tins
at his feet, the bus smelling of his tins.

slipping

I saw today the cars of a subway move, and behind
their accelerating bulk a creamy friction in the air,
like an almost transparent custard. What was it? Some
toxic flume from the mechanical contrivances of transport?
No. There is no visible exhaust from these underground
carriages. It was the cognitive stuffing of the people
on the train. Don't laugh! These trains accelerate
and the contents of our brains slip quietly out. It explains

the dull torpor we feel down there. A lingering cloud of agitations,
fears, sexual longing, vanities, hopes, distractions. I think
I even saw tiny bugs feeding on the gauzy drift. Small speckled
beetles with black and white wings that hummed
ever so softly something modern while eating forgotten thoughts.
Actually, I was wrong. They were humming something very very old.

roofing

He sits — a significant weight, then rubs
his knees with two palms, small pressured
circles, and he rocks slightly, and I rock

slightly, watching my father touch his body
in this small, tender way. I'm trembling
a little, and the sun is trembling into the moss

and ferns through the trees. My brother
hands me roofing tar and we pack it around
old crumbling bricks, rebuilding them with zeal

and too much tar. We are on the roof
of the cottage. My father no longer comes to these heights.
He rubs his knees and looks around, sighing at a planet

that has grown 'round him for 72 years, blinking up
at sons who are strangers, who grew to men slowly,
almost like the ferns that never seem to change,

like the sunlight and lake water. My need has changed.
And as he rubs his knees, he needs these two men,
my brother and me, clumsy with words,

better with roof tar than affection.
But the roof tar is affection, we are
doing something, stopping leaks around an old

crown, trembling a little, watching
from a height a man puzzled by the brevity
of his life.

I was only passing. Actually, I was in a rush

It was the way her thighs looked in the light,
and the way the ambulance flickered,
and the man in the crowd, about her age,
how he jammed his hands in his pockets

hard and moaned a little, angrily, helplessly,
her ample girth spread on the cement step,
the awful ruined geometry of collapse.
It was his cane and his business shirt and his slacks,

still crisp at that late hour, the way his cane
marked an uneven retreat. And then her horrible
cry when they moved her body, how a body resists
and collapses with a million little shifts.

I was only passing. Actually, I was in a rush,
racing from one place and eager for the next,
convincing myself that when my legs fuck-off
to some other part of the night,

when I fall on the stairs, when the terrible rebellion
of bones truly begins, the howl I will hear
like the one I heard as I moved away will really be
the drunk pleasure of the young on a hot Montreal night.

And if a crowd has gathered (as no doubt it will,
it always does) the best that have gathered
will have come — not to see — but to stamp their foot
at old age and spit at the unfairness. In short,

although I can't prove this, it was clear to me
that we were all falling, even as I passed,
and that no one was sure, and we were almost
embarrassed — we were so close,

we could have touched, if we wanted.

cradle and light

The cradle of the train rocking through the dusk.
I am going to see my father who has had a stroke.
Dirty rows of corn zipper past, and the white roofs
of farms hover over fields in the weakening light.
Solitary trees stand crooked over empires of bales
faltering to ash. In the August heat this ripened landscape

is like an image in a still pond. Inside the train
children pass back and forth in the aisle. Something
about them seems to slow the light, make the day
linger and resist the shadows seeping in from the fields.
Maybe it's the laughter or the whimsical screaming,
but even they can't make it stop, and soon the train

is lit from within. I can see its glow flickering past
on the ground in the dark beside the sway-and-rap
of axles and wheels. And now, the children have stilled.
The faces of their parents are bent on seats,
even they glow a little, the air filmy with their sleep.
The train is like a moon gliding past farmhouses

in the dark, a memory of laughter that briefly
held the light — its cargo the uneasy dreams dreamed
between the places we must get to, and leave.

MICHAEL LITHGOW was first attracted to poetry in high school, a lucky accident of curriculum that celebrated the work of American poet William Carlos Williams. Born 1965 in Ottawa, he changed cities many times during his early years, living in Halifax, Burlington, Memphis, Brantford, Edmonton, and Saskatoon. In the mid-1980s Michael moved to Vancouver, where he was active in the media arts through freelance writing, community radio and television, local theatre, and readings. Before returning to school to pursue studies in journalism and communications, he worked for nine years as a paralegal specializing in First Nations law. Michael remains active in media arts as a contributing editor at ArtThreat.net, research associate at Open-Media.ca and director at Cinema Politica. He is currently a Ph.D. student in the School of Journalism and Communication at Carleton University, exploring the relationship between aesthetics and knowledge. Since 2005 he has lived in Montreal. Cormorant will publish his first poetry collection in 2012.

George Pakozdi

Nine Poems

Homesickness

She left behind everything:
rain, ubiquitous as the sound
of bullets, those sharp exhalations
among the banana leaves, air that pours off
the coastal mountains like incense, heavy
smells of foods whose names exist
only in the regional dialect,
the city's colourful mazes negotiable
by the initiated, the street vendor slogans,
political graffiti, clanging of pots
in orchestrated protest and slums
that spill down the hills
like waterfalls.

She left these behind in exchange
for quiet. For a country of peaceful
suburbs. A measured vernacular.
A diaspora of importers and restaurant owners
bringing in all the correct ingredients
or their closest substitutes.
For a reconstituted home. To play,
on anemic winter afternoons,
a CD mimicking the explosions
of rain against a skylight.

A Promise

One day we'll go.
We'll dig our silverware and our ancestral
coat of arms out from under the floorboards,
pack our dictionaries, scribble down one
or two recipes in the shorthand of our village.
Each of you can bring a favourite toy.
We'll wait for a festival or a riot
in the capital and then slip out
past briefly-vacated border posts.
The world will open loving arms. Everywhere
they sympathize with our cause. One day
you will learn a new anthem
and a new set of slogans, the rules
of foreign games, a million ways to fill your free
time. I'll show you how to create
miniature governments in exile
with your friends, the children of other
émigrés, with whom I'll converse
loudly in public about the smuggled-out reports
of a place that does not change,
a place that no longer sustains us.
One day the secret police will creep
through the plumbing of this old house
and find nobody to spy on.

Abandoned House

The house in the photo sits alone on scrubby
rural land. It looks shy and somehow naked,
or rather the inverse of naked — stripped
inside of furniture, walls shedding their wallpaper
like rejected skin grafts. The house is sad
and wants to creep away from the photo's centre,
but the camera pins it there, forcing everything
else to the margins: the tire-tracked snow on the road,
the slanted telephone pole, the trees'
crooked upward yearning. We are permitted
to consider these things only in the context
of the house they surround. Their individual
histories float somewhere outside the frame. Someone
must have lived in the house, neighbourless, sweeping
the needles from the small ponderosa
off the front steps. A young couple with a baby,
perhaps. She on maternity leave, he
a freelance journalist who's used the money
from the advance on his first book to move
the family into a two-bedroom condo far away
from the little house in the snow. Or maybe
it is wrong to assume the house abandoned. Maybe
since the photo was taken it has been bought
and painted, new shingles tacked on, cracked front door
replaced. Maybe the couple still lives there
and they're happy and get woken up every morning
at four by the baby, and when she's old enough
they'll decorate the pine with lights and little paper angels
and she'll stay up all night on Christmas Eve,
staring out past the branches.

November 4th, 2006

Fifty years ago you stand staring hopeful
at the sky, breathing cold air
on the banks of the Danube
as its frozen surface refracts the moonlight.
If the onslaught comes tonight, do you stay
or divide the pigs, gather your children on your back,
disappear into the snowy countryside?

That beast, jointed like a centipede, scuttles
towards Budapest on a million legs,
to swallow the city in its clanging jaws.
Your cousins prepare to test brick
and bone against steel and rubber tread.

I wish I could reach back through
the quiet decades and relieve the weight for you —
you, who could balance me standing on your palm
as a child; you already an old man then,
whose life was defined by that sleepless night
spent listening for the echoes of a million boot falls.

Nana's 90th Birthday

In your honour we're all drunk by five.
The day is overcast but the house is lit up
with noise, guests having swept in
from all the dim crawlspaces of your life.
We span four generations and would like
some day to be as old as you. Our gifts
are bright and obscenely textured.
We line up to present them, holding your hand
and basking in the closeness of your world.
The toasts start, progressively louder
and more inane and heartfelt, we interrupt
and are interrupted, someone pours another
round of drinks. An uncle knocks his over
and you ask who it was. Everybody laughs.
He kisses you between the wrinkles
on your forehead and we dissipate
into conversation, Irish dancing lessons,
spontaneous arm-wrestling tournaments
and carpeted-stair bum races.
An eighty-seven year old woman lectures
on Sarasota social life and vacuums gin.
A little cousin sneaks a taste
and spits it out. His sister has gotten in
to the fur closet and is dragging
a huge beaver coat around the house, chased
by the dog. At the center of all this your eyes
are red-rimmed and glassy, your mouth
etched into a smile. Someone puts up
vacation pictures on the TV and you
are radiant, pretending to see.

Some things I did not say to my grandmother while helping her move into Highgate Retirement Community

"Look nana you've got the biggest TV in the place,
dad and I could barely carry it and almost dropped it
on its screen spilling plasma everywhere and staining
the carpet in high-definition — yeah I know you don't understand
lines of resolution or contrast ratios but I promise
if it wasn't for your cataracts you'd appreciate the technology.
Lucky you all the single old men will be coming by your
room which reminds me my friend works at a retirement home
and said the residents have sex all the time ('just a little
more slowly'), there are even retirement home sluts,
which I'd rather not think about but I guess I find reassuring.

"Frankly I'm terrified by the nameplates on the doors,
by the shapeless, sagging bodies, by the stench
of baby powder and urine floating in the halls.
I'm thinking of hitting the panic button next
to your bathtub so I can escape in the disturbance —
this place reminds me of a university residence
with a funeral home aesthetic and I know
you're scared too, you keep glancing nervously
at the photos of my sister and me as if you may not
see them tomorrow and you're gripping my hand extra tight
as you forget the same old stories into my chest.

"I can understand why you'd be anxious about climbing
into the last bed you'll ever sleep in
and making some new mummified friends,
but at least the meals here are good and the flowers
are always fresh — oh wait, they're plastic,
people must have allergies."

ONLINE STUDY: Have You Survived War and/or Sexual Violence?

Welcome. The bare modernism and stained
particle-board library carrels of academia

may have something for you. Your stories are important
for our research. We can offer psychological services

and enter your name in the draw for an iPod.
We understand that it may be difficult

to talk about: take your time. You can save
and return whenever you'd like.

Step outside and have a cigarette. Call one
of your surviving relatives back home

or take your children to the movies.
The one about dogs is quite charming. We can wait.

But please, do finish the survey. We need your help
to better understand what's going on

in the data we've collected.

The Border

Just across the border
there is another town,
similar in size to this one,
full of seedy motels
and the kind of disreputable men
who are attracted
to borders. For whom proximity
is replete with opportunity.
Corrupt bureaucrats, hired guns, traffickers
in drugs and stolen laptops
and human beings. Across the border,
the houses are built the same
as here, wrought-iron balconies
and facades painted in pastels,
though the shutters
tend to be closed and shabbier
and the avocadoes grown
in the courtyards smaller, more sour.
If you climb the hill on the edge
of town on a clear day
you can see their roofs glinting.
A taxi driver will take you across
and speak to the border guard,
in the regional dialect, for a tip.
A carton of cigarettes makes a good
substitute for a visa.
The people there are humourless
and xenophobic. You can't trust them.
They are endlessly devaluing
their currency against ours
and extorting our merchants
for tariffs. They practice
rituals similar to our own
but with strange, pagan twists;

devil-worship is said
to be rampant.
From the hill at night
you can see the glow
of their stolen electricity,
you can hear their orgiastic revelry,
the phantom screams
of human sacrifices. Be careful.
Turn off your flashlights.
For all we know
they could have agents out there
in the borderlands,
watching us.

Twice-Bombed

> *"I could have died on either of those days. Everything that follows is a bonus."*
>
> – Tsutomu Yamaguchi, the only officially recognized survivor of both the Hiroshima and Nagasaki atomic blasts (d. 2010, age 93). *The New York Times*, January 6, 2010

To wake up in the hospital and stretch your arms gingerly
above your head and think of yesterday, a bonus.

To listen to the cries for rescue echoing among the buckled houses,
to feel the heat of the individual fires chasing each other

from stovetop to collapsed timber to orange grove, a bonus.
To reach down and pull a burned woman from the rubble by the hand

and feel her skin slip off like a glove; to rinse
the eye sockets of the soldier who had been monitoring the sky

of their sticky fluid. To dig up the potatoes baked in the ground
by the heat of the explosion and have lunch. A bonus,

to take the train home to Nagasaki
and live the devastation an absurd second time:

the same noiseless white flash, the same upward column of debris,
the same rationing of bandages and separation of the savable

and the not-savable. A bonus, everything. To recover
from your flesh wounds. To live the banality of a long, quiet life

and to die at an old age, under normal
conditions of discomfort.

GEORGE PAKOZDI grew up in Hamilton, Ontario, where he was born in 1987. His paternal family moved to Canada from Hungary following the 1956 revolution. On his Toronto-born mother's side, his roots go back to England and Scotland. George currently lives in Toronto with his wife, Maria. He began writing after graduating high school, having been introduced to the possibilities offered by poetry in Mrs. Kearns-Padgett's Advanced Placement English class. Allen Ginsberg was an early influence. Currently George is completing the M.A. in English and Creative Writing at the University of Toronto, where he has been fortunate to work with A.F. Moritz, Jeff Parker, Rosemary Sullivan, and mentor Ken Babstock. The university's teaching assistant positions, scholarships and bursaries, workshops, and student publications have offered him constant opportunities to pursue his writing. George has spent the past few summers traveling in Europe and North and South America. His poetry is inspired by family history, travel, popular culture, and borders of varying types and permeability.

E. Alex Pierce

Seven Poems

Boat

The water went by in deep swirling spirals from the oars. The boat passed over the channel, over the eel grass feathering and quickening. It was no good trying to be good, there was no good. And if I don't write it down it will not be written down. It will be lost in the fighting and taking and misery and hatefulness that surrounds us and eats us from childhood and sorrow.

There will be no more voice of the grandfather, the father, calling the channel, knowing its name. Salt sea water entering the river. Opening its way in from the ocean, when the sea was mystery and clean, larger than us, plain.

Because we are not ourselves — ourselves in the boat, moving on the water in perfect peace. We are late for supper, and there is no one home.

In the Sand Hills

Down in the dunes is a language place, lost U-vowel of the sound turned round,
guts of the rabbit strewn over ground. Grit of the fir cones, peeled by squirrels.

No one is here. Shadow of a lost imagined pony skin, lichen scab
creeps over the dune ridge. Trees, grown up, grown over, an acre of sand.

Layer of forest floor, tangle of alder — closing the pathways. Tongue
of cold sand, far up inland, a half mile from shore — I want it back.

I want it all clean. I want Mozart in a piano-echoed room, scales in thirds.
I want my mother making shapes of everything, poems in thin air —

my father singing hymns in the car all the way from Sable River
to Liverpool — Hunt's Point, Summerville, and Port Mouton.

I want to be always in that car when we slow down for the turn
at Robertson's Lake — that big rock ledge *with the lemonade springs*

where the bluebird sings — the *Big Rock Candy Mountain.* I want to be
in that clear, sweet space. I want to write my poems then,

grow up again, breathe in that clean, light air. I want to have
my babies then, take them to the Sand Hills, stay

in that sheltered place. I want my clear syllables to drop
on that sand. I want the rain to pelt down our bareback skins

as we ride those pretend ponies, my sister and I,
over the high, white dunes.

I want to speak the sounds I was born to speak —
be the music that played me, safe in that car

as we rolled down the clay-backed road that followed the river
down the flat salt marsh to the edge of the grandmothers' country.

I want not to have lost what I am looking for now. My sounds
are down there, back in those dunes, down at the cold green edge

where we slid down the hot, white sand into the cool
damp gray, where roots began — and alder intersected,

hid the trails that only rabbits crossed — the place
the tangle started. I want to lie back there

until the words form in my mouth
out of my land and my ground,

my crying places — my self, simple.
Not even happiness —

a bark, a yell, an arc of singing —
a breath. A sound —

is it over — all that over?
Is that where my child, daughter, would have gone —
she too, over?

This is so bare —

bare as a bone —

a bone of childhood.

If you could find your own small bone.

To float, to drown, to close up, to open up — a throat

where the great artery rises and crosses, coming so close
to the larynx, the lynx in larynx, the animal voice
in its first low growl —

Over the kitchen table, night, after lamp is lit, voices
of the grandmother and grandfather lifting into the low beams
of the small old house, the pitch rough —

Under the low roof in the attic above we can hear them
after we stop giggling. Together we shut out
the fear of the dark. The black so black,
nights with no moon. The beds so deep we drift
down to sleep. Into feathers and flannel —

their sounds lifting and falling,
pitched low, a mixture of stove black and coal tar,
hardwood and well water, its taste startling
cold, up out of the ground. The sounds
coming into us — into me. The green painted table,
curved chair backs, the brown teapot, cracked and porous —
Still there — grandfather's axe, biting
into the root of the apple tree blown over by wind: *There's life in it yet.*
Haul it back up. The oxen, the ropes, the straining — August apples,
Yellow Transparents, the best ones, worth saving.

The things that enter you before you know you're
breathing in — the things that grab hold of the voice box,
climb up into the throat — Sound of the pig squeal
muffled, shut out, morning of the pig death, the cauldron
prepared, great vat of scalding water, the kids all sent down the hill
to play by the shore — The scream, the blood — Was there a shot?
Heard or imagined, which is worse —

The sound of crab apples running down the chute to the pig's trough —
only yesterday — and milk, a bucket of milk and slop for the hungry,
vociferous sow — clean sided, white and pink, bright eyed,
sweet. Down by the river shore, the dragonfly with its darning needle —
It will come and sew up your mouth — lighting on the river rocks,
landing on some kid's arm. The river water soft — half fresh,
half salt — It tastes so good in your mouth. Cadence coming with the tide,
turning tongue of the tidal river lifting the small soft fragments of rock,
each piece worn, flat — tiny pieces stuck to the soles of your feet. Lap
of the arriving water pressing into the shore, the river's edge graduated,
sheltered — its language erasing now, the sounds civilized, modulated —
sound of the lawn mower — old sharp scrape of the whetstone
waiting in its can of rusty water to edge and hone the scythe.
Language tied to the land — translated, embedded,
repeated, remembered, half lost — The crab apples
all run over the ground. Worms in them, sow bugs
in the fence posts, thousands of shingle flies.

The slain pig, white carcass stretched from a rafter
in the dim, forbidden barn —

Common Loons

We are in the feather bed, thirteen, so close
our nightgowns touch. You have bangs cut
straight across. Downstairs we danced from
the moment the Victrola needle pricked. June roses
from the field outside in every glass tumbler
we could find. The parlour in this abandoned house
contains our crazy dancing. There's a dusty rug,
Aunt Mabel's choice, flowers in swirls, and ball fringe
on the horsehair furniture. It is almost pain, waiting
for the needle to come down. Then the rough scratching
while it searches for the groove. As we go round, waltzing
in each other's unaccustomed arms, the Charge of the Light
Brigade reverses and swings in its frame on the wall.

Their bayonets are ready. Their tall hats and bright braid
look almost foolish on that battleground. Lined up,
lined up. And death will come. In bed, we hear the
loons, late, over Johnson's Pond. Their night-hoots
follow the raccoon's squeal, the rats' rustling. We are
not afraid. Something deep, sweet, and impossible
drifts toward the centre of the bed. The feathers
drown us. The common loon's un-common laughter
trills and spirals down our spines. *Cruising down the river*
sings the Victrola. But we are past that now, pulled
into the lake's depth, diving with the loons, necks stretched,
mouths open, eardrums closed. Twenty, thirty, years from now
you will come to my door with your ancient father and give me
a rose slip you have dug up from that field.

Shelter

We were there in that dark with the bleat
and the crying around us. I could still hear you,
in that other language, speaking to them, to the lambs.

I stood still and wouldn't move,
fearful to go and fearful to stay,
the storm's voice coming from without,
the animals' voice, within.

And I knew them, that they were safe now.

Then the luxury of the lambs came down,
and you were there where you wished to be,
upon me, rippling out and outer
with a sound of wind over wind and rain over rain,
of wool over wool and flesh over flesh,
the sound of a sound folding into itself,
until my bones were glad to be that frame
over which my skin, like a tent, had stretched itself.

Full Moon

When it's full moon on the Sable River bar, high tide is always eight o'clock —
her father gives her this, from Everett, his father. He gives her
the dog whistle, a canvas bucket, a new lawn mower, his breaking heart.
Nor' nor' east, nor' east, east nor' east — east. Boxing the compass.
East sou' east, sou' east — he stands in the kitchen of the new house
he built so long ago. He is ending, can't do the woods-work
anymore. Can't pile in the hardwood they need for winter. His old language
coming back — *Wood for winter, hoe potatoes, haul the eelgrass, brace the shed.*

She drives his truck and runs it off the icy road. Rolls it. *This was my life,*
he says — *my life.* A bucket full of sorrow. Pays someone to haul the truck
away, repair it, keep it. Over. The way they tell their stories. Plain.
Heroes in this place of river tide and ocean storm, of deer kill and
wild-goose, wild cat and porcupine. His Christmas tree lot, the poison
used to kill the maples killing him. His measure
over every acre of his land — lengths still counted out
in chains. His steady cadence, how that falls
and wraps her. No more sorrow, no.

Twig and fire and breath of wind —
window's rattle. The end of him.

≈

The Sable River empties into the bay, running westward onto Louis Head.
It splits its channel either side of John's Island, touches the Ferry Lane
on the east — our side — then mingles with the sea salt water,
reaching almost to the creek. The sand bars make a backbone
up the bay, and seals come in to lie there. Once
I found a seal pup on the shore, alive and hissing.

Before there was the bridge, upriver, people used to holler to the ferryman
to row the dory over and take them back and forth. And now
the bridge is gone, the pilings left, our Ferry Lane a small path
through the woods that runs down to a sheltered beach.
And who can find the path our mothers took us to —
and named it. (We thought it meant the *fairy* lane.)

My father knew the names of every one in every house,
West side, East side — up and down the Sable River. Foss Lisk's place
opposite his house, where Blanche would watch, and phone up
when she saw their car come in the yard. *I've been looking for your light.*

A signal, when night was black and full moon an event
that every creature waited for. To hunt, or hide, or plot,
or seize, or court. Full moon late in August. Cut the alders,
take a run down to the beach to see the moon come straight up
from the water. Like the first time, the only time. Breakers
rolling in — the ancient sound of breath upon a rock.

Vox Humana

The thing which has no voice,
refuses to speak, is a thing
flayed and pitiless. It will
survive, it will swim

through the passages and corridors
of its undertaking.
It will name itself vagrant,
subordinate, unfledged, vestigial

faultless, sweet — until it strike
by accident or design, a surface
abrasive, unreflective,
which does not require beauty.

Feeling the probe of its fish-nudge,
floating in a current at last
recognizable, it will sing to itself,
I am, I am

misshapen, unlovely, unadorned,
unknowable —
disjunctive, implacable, illicit,
unreasonable —

feral, wily,
free.

E. ALEX PIERCE lives in what used to be her grandmother's house in East Sable River, Nova Scotia, not far from Liverpool where she grew up. Writer, mentor, editor, and cross-disciplinary artist, she began as a musician, studying piano at Mount Allison University, then served a theatre apprenticeship in London, England. She worked at Canadian Players, Shaw Festival, the Vancouver Playhouse, Kaleidoscope Theatre, and the National Arts Centre. Her theatre and dance work includes more than twenty original solo and collaborative performance works presented in venues across Canada. While serving as Theatre Awards Officer at the Canada Council (1985–92) she began writing as an outgrowth of dream-work in Jungian analysis. In 1993 Alex entered the writing program at Warren Wilson College, graduating with her MFA in 1997. She has been a member of the Banff Centre's Writing Studio and Banff Wired Writing, and has been published in journals and anthologies in the US and Canada. For ten years she taught creative writing at Cape Breton University, and is currently Series Editor for The Essential Cape Breton Library. Brick Books will publish her first poetry collection, *Vox Humana*, in the fall of 2011.

Jason Ranon Uri Rotstein

Eight Poems

The Boat

We are on a boat,
Without anchor.
Though a captain may deem us unfit to sail,
We resolve to teeter between death and quick surrender;
No crewmen to mend and render our sails;
No one but our own — .

And so we dip in again: tumble and crash.
No settlement to anchor our waves;
No certain — destination.
We navigate — as it were —
Blind.

What we do we can learn from no one — no woman, no man.
No one has yet been this far before.
We cannot expect to repeat a voyage;
No voyage here is done again.

When we pray, we pray that our voyage does not desert us;
That we do not limit our hearts;
That we trust each other above ourselves;
And that we will still wake up on that day and love:
The rock and the swig of the person lying next to us — again.

Blow wind in their hair — these travellers —
Blow wind in their hair

We are always first-time travellers,
And our boat is as yet unnamed.

Groundswell

She struck me as a sail
Perpendicular to land
That flapped and paled in the wind
Grounded, upended, creased
I had her bent over a chair
I was her ship, her captain, her wind
Her everything, her god — dare say that —
She put everything into my hand
And for no price she made this small little man
Petty in his conceits, a dove
A duke of this land
It was a power I could not sublimate or control
Neither wanting, nor knowing how to do unto her differently

Before & After

We made the mistake
> Of fighting before we were properly engaged
>> And the mistake of talking about marriage

When we never kissed
And we still haven't kissed
> And all that time we spent together
>> And that night we spent all-night-together

When we wouldn't go to bed together
When we took turns petting the cat
While it purred in its sleep on the floor
And we slowly closed our eyes and went to sleep
> And then we made the mistake of dreaming together

And when we woke again in the morning
> The mistake of cooking together
>> The mistake of experimenting with ingredients

And our friends called us passive-aggressive like a married couple
> And we made the mistake of loving each other

> Before and after our time was up.

Most Wanted

She tries to dress down. She tries to disguise my like.
To sign my retreat with demonstrations of a different sight.
She tries to stymie my intent, stymie my heart,
Exhort and signal my retreat with allusions to an advancing fight:
All to get me to go away.

Truthfully, she charms me.
Not cuckolds me, with stories,
Past histories of other men — older and bigger — on her side.
She is silly. The way she wavers with my hope.
The way she gets louder and louder; the way she squeals; then screams.
The way she stays silent and you can hardly hear her. I don't take cover.
She tries to soil hate. She tries to displace my like.
She likes to invent new religions for me to discover — at another location.
So I've caught on.

She tries to tell me she is at the end of her rope.
She tries to bargain with me: *As if one kiss were ever enough.*
She tries to kiss me off, not kiss me; elude me, not elope with me.
She tries to disguise my like. To dress down:
Burn away fake, imagined brushes against fabrics: Hers.
Burn silks, felts, flannels. Anything that feels soft. — Chenilles.
Infuse the air with faulty smells I don't know.
I play dummy.

She tries to disguise my like in tough
Brown corduroy that doesn't come close
To the brown paper bag she's trying to impersonate.
I see clear now. It's part of what can be appreciated.
She leaves much to the imagination.

To get close to her I might prod from afar.
She is fragile, close to fight, easily broken.
To get close I might prod from afar.
First with a cane then a hand. I am not an old man.
All associations are changed when she is around.
When she steps to the room, I might prod from afar.
Maybe a cane. Then a hand. She tries to dress down.
She shines through.

No Great Artist

By now, she is well past her literary prime
But she never had one

She never retired like Bellow in his old age
Now and then, I receive one of her letters

I hope you are well and settling in and getting into the routine.
It was so great hearing your voice yesterday like sun shine coming through
the telephone.

She still writes in longhand
On fine stationery left over from one of mom's affairs

I saw Mom and Dad yesterday — they were just back from Montreal and L.A.
The house is empty — just Sam. She will have to get used to it.

With none of that abiding care for diction, syntax and grammar
Her style is best described informative

You ask me, she leaves Hemingway in the dust
Pushing the sentence to new extremes

For you it is a total new experience but a great one. We are so lucky to have
enjoyed each other, the lunches, the movies, etc. — just to enjoy our talks —
time together.

Unvarnished short declarative sentences
Just a free-associative string

I will try to mail this today if I can get out.
Please excuse the shaky handwriting.

Complete with cross-outs and slanting lines
But I think she manages very well in all

I love you. Look after yourself.
Will write again.

I find my grandmother's shaky cursive
                                Reads best in low light
Wherever   Painful red eyes contract.

Science Experiment

He used to stand over me, recite the words as if from a tape.
When he neared his end, he tired and tried to close early.
No applause. (This was not his work. It was mine.)
I quoted his fault. He had gone this far already. *Why not farther?*
He dictated to me a few words at a time as if to his Dictaphone.
All punctuation observed. Night by night I readied the pencil.
Frisked my ears to catch the last gasp. I closed in on the spelling
And strove to process the letters in unison, together.

He set up my project, I knew, *as he would.*
He didn't have much time for this; yet he had an unusual amount to say.
Nothing could be left to chance.
Frequently he closed in on a word. He asked for my quiet.
He closed his eyes and rolled back his head.
He encircled around me. Ceremoniously. He told me to write faster.
I tried to get a word in, suggest a new tack.
He sat beside me. He requested more light.
Leaned in. *Do you see what you're doing?*
I can't write straight. He is the exacting one.
He came up with the experiment.
He brought home the information.
I did what he did. I replaced him.

Doing Away with the Heart
(for Nuala Ní Dhomhnaill)

Do away with the heart
Move the centre out to the periphery
Cut away, cut in, divide the fat from the bacon
And see what is left over
Make what is left whole
Let the sea come in and fill the void

Do away with the heart
Cover it over
With what remains makeover
To the occasional maudlin fancy
Slide ruler in and under
To see what is left over
Seal off the collective
In the inner earth
And keep the communal tide from
Rushing through
Hands hold the key to the heart
And with these hands bury all
Meaning whole
Knockabout here, knockabout there
Take a feeling without weight, a pure
Morsel without sugar
Win the salt away with sugar
And win the way out
From the uncovered hole
The heart is shattered
And in it are pieces of us all

Do away with the heart
It is my secret
What wounds this flimsy string holds
And time is too heavy
Hear it pounding, rousing from beneath the earth
Heavy, heavy in its stammering
Do not forget yourself

Frame

This I pick up and use to my own ends
Here I let fly, here I let bat against the wind
Here I abandon logic in numbers
Here I let risk the confusion of orientation
Here I let you walk me back on my way

This I indoctrinate in full step
Here I let take full wing
Here I skip by twos to haywired branches
Here I let go farther from sublunar reality
Here I desist from a plan; here I go the long way back down

This frame I let fall away

~

JASON RANON URI ROTSTEIN began writing poetry as the proper prerequisite for writing fiction; it has since become a lifelong pursuit. Born in Buffalo, New York (1984) and raised in Toronto, Jason has spent significant time abroad, in England, Ireland and Iceland. He obtained an A.B. (Phi Beta Kappa; Cum Laude) from Cornell University and M.A. (Merit) from the University of Sussex. His publishing record began in his early twenties with publication of his first poems in the *Literary Review of Canada* and *PN Review* (UK). He has since served as a Commonwealth Scholar in England, a Visiting Scholar at Massey College, a Research Associate at the Northrop Frye Centre of Victoria College at the University of Toronto and as a Visiting US-Fulbright/Icelandic Government Scholar at the University of Iceland. He serves as Poetry Editor of the *Jewish Quarterly* and as an Associate Editor for *Kilimanjaro: Creative Art and Design*. His book reviews appear regularly in such places as *The Globe and Mail* and *Canadian Literature*.

Kay Weber

Ten Poems

Some Functions of a Canoe

with a nod to Some Functions of a Leaf by Don MacKay

To wend. To lengthen wandering
into whole days and slow nights.

To turn and return, bog and sail,
lug cargo and carry,
huff and slop over rough water,

to remember muscle and bone
   curve of rib
   arc of pelvis
the slap lap of wavelets
licking a shoreline. To smell desire

in the suck and drag of deep,
to hear sleep, a forest silent, to find

re-splendour

to remember love.

Sunday School Acrostic

Jesus first
Others second
Yourself last

The order of things was in the code of labour:
corn rows turned tight at the end of the field,

the garden sewn together with hoe stitches,
the cellar room straight, shelves and bright jars.

Lord, preserve us from want,
bless this food to our bodies

that we may serve you.
Desire sealed with a boiled lid clamped hard,

the house scoured daily, sweet buns baked and broken
for a round of chores and Sunday singing.

We were baptized with sweat long before
they tipped the pitcher to mark us with water

in the name of the Father and Son and
the Holy Ghost, that faint friendly shadow.

Dairy Farm (Waterloo County, 1963)

O worship the Lord in the beauty of holiness
 — The Mennonite Hymnal

The hands of milkers knew the heft of flesh,
the squeeze of teat, the pressure of filled skin.
Their palms were cups, curved like the yowls
of barn cats twining their ankles
when the spray hit the pail with a pointed hiss.

Those men knew quiet,
the herd in their stanchions,
the sweet musk of hay and rustle of cud,
forehead pressed to flank, hands working the udder,
the let-down, the warm trickle —

Quiet of the night-stilled morning
in farmhouse kitchens, too,
where rockers creaked,
babies milking their mothers.

Calling Back Home
Southern Ontario, 2005

History repeats. Coyotes are sighted
at my parents' farm. Strange dogs
running across the south field.

A curled, yellowed memory
detaches itself from the West,
my father's birthplace.
It floats across his weakening vision.

The night-dog cry unnerves my mother,
born on this farm.
It wakes her memory of free running
red fox and the reassuring terror of
gunshot shattering.

My mother hums at breakfast
blessed assurance, Jesus is mine.
Beyond the window
my father whistles off-key
*Saviour like a shepherd lead us
much we need thy tender care,*
the old farm dog heaves himself to his feet
wags his tail in half time.

Lately I've been trying to talk to my parents
about how it really is for me —

but it comes out as a howl
launched from somewhere
beyond the circle of homelight,
strange-throated, toothy.

I fray their blessed assurance,
stir up their wild dog past.

In a Season of Not Belonging

The feeling of being lost
from your family
is sewn into your bones,
must have been there all along.

You apply patches and rags
to swaddle the ache,
but it's no use, they
keep unwinding.

All your efforts, little or big,
to tell the right stories,
bring home the right flowers
have now come to this:

you must rip the rags
from their place
and hang them like flags
in a new country.

The Other Congregation

This is my story, this is my song,
Praising my Saviour all the day long.
— The Mennonite Hymnal

The men at the hostel next door to the church
cough all day long.
This is their story, this their song,
a phlegmatic conviction.

From my kitchen window I mark these —
uneasy neighbours measuring their days
by the offices of their various devotions.

Hour by hour the men bow
over cupped hands and matchbook fires,
praising small flames and cigarettes.
They lean their ears toward AM radio
taking turns tuning the station:
gospel, country, old rock.

Saturday nights they smoke smuggled pot,
hiding their half-finished joints by the church door
under the lit-up leaves of the cropped spirea,
loping away on their funny strides when
they hear someone coming.

Sunday mornings they stay inside,
ducking the congregation.
Once a month, a lady from the church
brings them a cake.

What Was But Now is Lost

Un-married
unwife sorts marriage rot,
what is left of love from untruth
no small matter,
unlove, how unlovely.

Unhusband goes,
woman then unwoman
unhouseowner, unyoung,

Mother, then unmother,
unchildren grow and leave
white beds unmade —

    Remember the long green days
        and the butterfly that lit
            on the brown-eyed boy's shoulder?

Unlover,
remember the uncat, the undog,
the unwhite picket fence

still unlatched.

Dropping Amy Off to Go to China

She says I need to talk to you
as we haul her suitcase pillow rolled
sleeping bag and sack of snacks
from the trunk   I realize she packed
for this trip on her own
I didn't even do the laundry
She walks ahead of me toward the bus
then turns and says I am seriously
in love with him Mom and we
hug goodbye what else is
there to do?
                As I drive toward
home in the almost dawn a flickering
streetlamp bursts into bloom.

Notes from the Physical World
to the lost children

Wherever you are,
this is what has been happening in your absence:

there are four who made it through.
Grown now, mostly.

As I write this, two should be boarding the plane
for far away, if all goes well at the airport

(airports were kinder places
in your brief day).

The other two have returned from travels,
left again and returned again,
returned and kept on leaving.

Your father and I left each other long ago.

Even if you had made it,
you two would have been alone here now,

with me.

Sum

Sometimes a life
is more than the sum of its
cuts and bruises, more
than the sum of its success.
What is a soul's net worth?

Some days you turn a corner
and before you a scrap of field
unfolds in a green you had forgotten,

you turn a corner and
a streetscape surprises —
the slope of a red roof over a small window,
the blue painted door,
the black iron knocker.

Every now and again
you travel without intention
and the stranger face suddenly appears
human as your own.

KAY WEBER was born in 1959 on a farm in the heart of Ontario's Waterloo County Mennonite community, and lived in Mennonite communities in Virginia and Ohio before returning to the farm in the early 1970s. Both parents served as pastors; her grandfather was song leader, and helped compile a hymnal. Words were plentiful in her culture but people didn't like to waste them: this was a problem for a talkative, imaginative child. In Kay's early years, "literature" was the Bible, hymns, memory verses, and the *Childcraft Encyclopaedia* — but she also read the garden, she read the barn and its animals. Of the first generation in her family to attend high school, she loved English and studied languages. Scholarships to study in France and at the University of Western Ontario brought her into what she thought was "the world"; reading literature according to Northrop Frye's paradigms was mind-altering. Finishing her degrees piecemeal while raising four children, Kay took the occasional poetry workshop and for seven years taught English at a Mennonite high school. She did not think to publish until a friend suggested she submit poems to *The New Quarterly* in 2005. Currently she teaches high school in Victoria, B.C.

Margo Wheaton

Two Poems

Seeing Me Home

What did the neighbours think?

Drifting by their windows,
going to check on the youngest,
maybe help with homework

or looking up during commercials
and gazing outside, the sitcom
still fresh

or nudging each other, eyebrows
up to the bottom of the blinds, motioning
Tell Mom, she's *gotta* come see this:

the boy with the bad reputation carrying
a girl unconscious in his arms.

Steady as a procession, he passes
beneath the eyes of the houses, blind
to the blue flicker of screens,
occupied with the task at hand:

her mouth open and oblivious
as an accident victim's,
bra strap showing, a sandal gone.

He carries her the way someone carries
a child to bed, breath-held careful
so as not to disturb any dreams,
incur cries.

Seen like this,
through the window of a poem
they could be a metaphor.

Could be Lear carrying Cordelia,
her body all our unanswered questions

or a man lifting his bride
over the threshold into the white room
of a new life

or Abraham bearing Isaac,
grim and beaten
but believing.

Believe me
they are none of these things.

This is just that goddamned Melanson kid
managed to get the whole neighbourhood high
lugging that Wheaton girl back to her father's place
been drunk since her mother left,
girl's not gonna make nineteen.

This is just the pain
in living, impossible to bear
and bodies bearing it.

Torn

(for Rhonda Bourgeois 1964–1992)

I

Then in the dark room
I opened my eyes, torn from a thick
batting of sleep without knowing
why, a rider thrown

clear of an ambling dream.

In the empty field of that hour, only
the sound of my father's snores
rolling back and forth across
the hall, dark

and satisfied.

It didn't let go, the feeling —
as though being broadcast through
air — that something was wrong

like when you suddenly wonder, miles
from home, if you turned off
the stove, if the door had really
locked behind you.

I went downstairs, encountered
the unconscious hum of the house.

Phlegmy mantra of the ancient fridge.
The static croon of stereo speakers
left on by mistake. From the porch,

the soft ruckus of summer air
trying to jimmy a patio door.

I checked every room, eventually
climbed the stairs resigned. Went numb
when I learned they'd estimated

his car had drifted into your lane,
sent you into the black-orange
of the collision

at four a.m.

the roar in your ears
as I was sitting at the kitchen table,
listening to the night's long turn

as if there was nothing
in the world but time.

II

We sat there in your mother's kitchen
the day after it happened
just feeling it

the slow drag of death

bowing the heads of your sisters.
All five arranged around the table
as if at a séance

staring ferociously into its centre.

(The youngest in a blue dress,
eight months pregnant
and inward, all that new life.)

Now and then,
our faces bobbed up

looked blankly at the others,
placed bits of conversation into
the air like decoys.

Your mother gave us
one good story:

She'd stayed out all night and this
would've been the third time in a row
or some foolish thing. Out running the roads

with that Jeffrey Melanson. Came waltzing in
at six in the morning lit up like a Christmas tree
singing John Prine, smelling like a brewery

and I said, "That's it. You're grounded."
She looked at me big-eyed as Bambi and said,
"Does that mean I can't go to the concert tonight?"

She slept most of that day then made up excuses
to enter whatever room I was in, go walking by me
real slow turning up her nose. I said, "You can act

like Lady Di all you like, my dear, but you're doing
it inside the house." Later, there was this lump
on her bed. (We all started to smile, knowing full well.)

Blankets done up like she was still there. Of course,
she picked the exact minute I ran upstairs to slip in
through the window, get under the covers.

She sat right up when I walked back in. Rubbed
her eyes and looked around confused, waking
up in the middle of the night and all, then said

in this pissed-off little voice, serious
as you please, "What are you doing up this late?
You should be in bed."

We sputtered with laughter then,
able to breathe. Straightened our backs
and gazed out the window, grinning

before the bulky silence
of your absence bowed
our heads back to the floor

firmly as a hairdresser's hands

and left us there,
chastised. Stuck.

III

Something funny
your mother insisted,
instructing me on the eulogy

your mother white with grief,
bone-white from the weight of it,
the living room a goddamn flower shop.

Just make sure you put something
funny in there.

Not much I could lift
from the way I found out,
on the phone with that RCMP officer:

This is one of the worst I've seen
and I've been looking at these things
for close to twenty years now. Both cars

just a ball of flames by the time I got there.
The guy's front end sitting right up
in her driver's seat. We're having trouble

identifying the passengers. Her sister thought
one of them might have been you.

Whatever sound I made
must have startled him then
because he stopped,

allowed a brief silence

and said

*In these things, it's the impact
that kills. I'm telling you*

she died just like that.

IV

Your eight-year-old daughter
left motherless.

She stands there
looking puzzled after they
tell her

cocks her head to one
side and says, astonished
at adult stupidity,

no.

That *couldn't* happen
to Mommy.

Already
a feel for narrative.

Squinting up, her face
seems to say let me
speak to the artist

in charge.

V

By the time evening
came, how the silence
had changed

a low Gregorian note
reaching through it,

singular

as the sick sense of timing
that tore you from your knowledge
of night, sudden glass, the blood's

journeying up and out.

You were driving across
the Cobequid hills on your way
back from Halifax, harbour city,

a symbol that fit you entirely,
friend, finally daring happiness at 28
like a stowaway.

The tenacity that steered you through
a childhood famous on our street
for its messy Dickensian plot

had served you like a guiding star
as you rowed against the expected
trajectory of your life.

Just weeks before, the social work degree
you'd earned in spite of your eighth-grade
education, the glowing allure of a desk,
decent pay cheque, the self-respect

of having eluded your little girl ghosts,
the ones that stalked you down the stairs even
after he was cast behind bars. *Dealt with.*

Telling me at the kitchen table
in my childhood home —

four doors and the length
of the ballfield from yours —

how you'd found it, the gold within

and me knowing the waves the rats the heat
you'd braved to get there. Rhonda,

you were lovely as sails

the last time I saw you. Casually
waving across one shoulder backing
onto the street and then pulling away.

Days later, Karen told me
your graduation ring was the only
thing belonging to you that had been
recovered.

How it must have looked
in the day's first light — like a secret
buried inside all that wreckage, whole

and shining.

MARGO WHEATON was born and raised in Moncton, New Brunswick. She attended Mount Allison University in her twenties, fell in love with the Sackville landscape, and completed a bachelor's degree with honours in English and Religious Studies. In the mid-eighties, she moved to Halifax where she wrote a thesis on socially outcast figures in Wordsworth's poetry and received a master's degree in English from Dalhousie. Margo's reviews and essays have appeared in *The Globe and Mail*, *The Fiddlehead*, *The Antigonish Review*, *Pottersfield Portfolio* and in Guernica Editions' *Series on Writers*. Her poems have been published in journals including *The Fiddlehead*, *The New Quarterly*, *The Antigonish Review*, and *Prairie Fire*, and in the anthologies *Landmarks: An Anthology of New Atlantic Canadian Poetry of the Land and Vintage 2000*. Her work received a High Commendation in the Petra Kenney competition and the Alfred G. Bailey award from the Writers' Federation of New Brunswick for best unpublished poetry manuscript. Margo works in Halifax as a freelance writer, editor and researcher for community-based organizations.

ACKNOWLEDGEMENTS ∽

E. Blagrave

"Past Tense," "The Sea Gull," "I have penny-weights," "Chestnut and Grey," and "You are so alone" appeared in *The Fiddlehead* in 1973. Much more recently, "Bipolarities" and "Tilt" appeared in *The New Quarterly*, and "Gatineau" in *Arc*.

Sarah Feldman

"Acheron" appeared in *The New Quarterly*.

Hamish Guthrie

"The Bubble's Hold" appeared in *The Malahat Review*, "Geography" in *Contemporary Verse 2*, "In Country Near Elora" in *The New Quarterly*; "The Afterlife" in *Prairie Fire*; "The Castle" in *Queen's Quarterly*; "A Road Near Kosovo" in *South Dakota Review*; "Night Fishermen on Bronte Pier" in *The Cape Rock*; "Noise" in *Poetry East*.

Amanda Jernigan

"Lullaby" and "Adam's Prayer" were first published in *Poetry*. "Lullaby" was subsequently published in *Poetry Daily* (on line); *Poetry Daily Essentials 2007*; *Jailbreaks: 99 Canadian Sonnets*; and *Alhambra Poetry Calendar 2010: Anthology*. "Marrying Days" and "Catch" were first published in *The New Quarterly*; "Memoir" in *Canadian Notes & Queries*; "Holy" in *Seven Mondays* and as a limited-edition broadside printed by Amanda Jernigan and John Haney and published under the imprint of Anchorage Press.

Daniel Karasik

"Conditions" appeared in *The Malahat Review*; "If carefully your father sat" appeared in *The New Quarterly*.

Michael Lithgow

"the desire of everything" appeared in *Bywords*; "I was only passing. Actually I was in a rush," "roofing," and "because of the light" in the chapbook anthology *Rutting Season: poetry & conversation* (Buffalo Runs Press, 2009). "slipping" appeared in *Arc*, where it was a finalist and an Editor's Choice in the 2010 Poem of the Year Contest; and "cradle and light"appeared in *The New Quarterly*.

George Pakozdi

"Twice-Bombed" appeared on line as a finalist in *Arc*'s Poem of the Year Contest 2010. An earlier version of "Abandoned House" appeared in *The Wa*.

E. Alex Pierce

"Boat" and "Full Moon" appeared in *Contemporary Verse 2*. "Shelter" appeared in *The Fiddlehead* (First Place, Fiddlehead Poetry Contest 1997). "Common Loons" appeared in *Arc*, as did a longer excerpt from "To float, to drown, to close up, to open up — a throat" (reprinted in *The Best Canadian Poetry in English* 2008).

Jason Ranon Uri Rotstein

"The Boat" appeared in *PN Review*; "Most Wanted" in *Stand* and *Literary Review of Canada*; "Before and After" in *Literary Review of Canada*; "Doing Away With the Heart" in *Salmagundi*; and "No Great Artist" in *Poetry Ireland Review*.

Kay Weber

"In a Season of Not Belonging" appeared in *Rhubarb*; "What Was But Now Is Lost" and "Calling Back Home" in *The New Quarterly*; "Some Functions of a Canoe" and "Notes from the Physical World" in *Contemporary Verse 2*, and "Dairy Farm (Waterloo County, 1963)" in *Arc*.

Margo Wheaton

"Seeing Me Home" was first published in *The Fiddlehead*.

ABOUT THE EDITOR ∼

ROBYN SARAH is the author of eight poetry collections, two collections of short stories, and a book of essays, *Little Eurekas: A Decade's Thoughts on Poetry*. Her poems have been anthologized most recently in *The Best Canadian Poetry in English* (2009 and 2010), *The Norton Anthology of Poetry*, Garrison Keillor's *Good Poems for Hard Times*, and *Modern Canadian Poets: An Anthology* (Carcanet, UK). Currently Poetry Editor for Cormorant Books, she lives in Montreal.

NEW POETRY FROM CORMORANT BOOKS

The Other Side of Ourselves
by Rob Taylor

Some frames
by Jack Hannan

No End in Strangeness:
New and Selected Poems
by Bruce Taylor